Praise for Dirty Words

There are forgettable words, there are memorable words and then there are dirty words. By dirty, I have found Sarah Lilius knows every kind of word (and emotion) out there, and is a master articulator, capable of threading together intoxicating poetry like a string of prayer beads. There's nothing sanitized in her intense soul, it's unfiltered all the way. If there were a new language, I would expect Lilius to have invented it. Her uncanny wielding of the nature of existence might well be written in blood; it's permanent, intoxicating, and shocking in its comprehension of us all. Dirty Words is as essential as eating, it doesn't need to beg, it summons, and you devour.

I'm drawn like prey to the intelligence and horror of Sarah Lilius's unveiling of life. She's wickedly uncanny in her knowledge of how to permeate our safe spaces and force us to think. Aside from being a striking modern poet with a shameless talent for edgy writing, Lilius may well be a phantom, haunting our collective subconscious, because she's got that gift for revealing what we didn't know ourselves, as if she's climbed inside our amygdala. Perhaps all great poets are slightly psychic, in that they act as harbingers for all that we feel and never admit we feel.

If your order is for a Sarah Lilius double-shot, extra strong, skip the cream, then you'll soon be a faithful regular.

Candice Louisa Daquin,
author of *A Jar For the Jarring*

Dirty Words: not just profanity slurred on the street, the phrases whispered under breaths, or inappropriate slang, but words that we pluck from the earth, words that we give power to and return these armored gems to our throats: they can be our mantra and protest, our resistance to a culture that wants to suppress our light.

Sarah Lilius writes about young girls, bears, bands, Barbie, boys in paneled wood basements, her poems like animals in the night: gritty, beautiful, lurking under the house long after they've murdered something small and soft and run into the forest. Lilius writes of a femininity that is strong and rakish, not afraid to murder but also pushing through to the end while trembling.

So many roles women play:

"At some point you are going to shower in a hotel bathroom," (Hotel Living)

"Girl, remember our heart is not there for others to eat." (Frightened Girl in the Circus)

"It's terrifying to cusp the spirits, to understand what isn't ever to be understood" (The Medium Begins Her Night)

"I line up boys in flannel, girl firing squad, self-control reeks of attitude and mint gum." (I Feel Stupid and Contagious)

What's Kurt without Courtney? In "Ode to Hole's Live Through This," Lilius captures the rage we own in moving our own bodies, stomping down indignities, any slight with heavy boots and sound. A reminder that we own this sound, always, tremors through the poem lines:

"*I rebel and put the wooden handled chopping knives in with the rest of the silverware. Courtney rotates and curtsies around the room I spend so much time in, she growls, screams like a hearty act of rebellion, a woman singing like that and a last name like Love, is singular yet plural, is a smudge, the whole canvas with paint left over for your face.*"

It is a blessing when we remember we are not alone in this world, that our voices and bodies seek and capture connection. We weave ourselves in and out of these poems and we connect: domestic, violent, specific and we escape though the exit, changed and stronger for it.

Lilius reminds us that we carve words out of stone every day. We surpass our comfort zones and fight back. We carry these rocks with us, for beauty, weaponry, to keep us grounded on the earth.

Jennifer McBain-Stephens,
author of *The Messenger Is Already Dead*

In *Dirty Words,* Sarah Lilius explores the female body in the world as animal, as object, as performance, as victim, as shame, as mother. These powerful poems inhabit a landscape lush with sex and music and bears and blood. They give us a history of girls and women who are "tired as buttons/used over and over," who are searching for "courage, an ashen/thing" anywhere it might hide: a forest, a circus, a hotel shower, a gravel road, a paneled basement, a kitchen with Hole blasting from the stereo, or on the edge of a cliff with Thelma and Louise. Using both narrative blocks and lyric fragments that call on both pop culture and the natural world, Lilius gives us a speaker who is a survivor, "with nothing inside or everything inside," arriving at last at the conclusion that "I'm the editor of my own heart."

Donna Vorreyer,
author of *To Everything There Is*

The aptly titled Dirty Words is akin to the risqué magazine hidden under your mattress or the diary of the coolest, most badass girl in school, who just so happened to be your mother. That is not to say that this collection centers on youth; it doesn't. Dirty Words follows its author through a rough and tumble life in which she vehemently questions the ongoing war between men and women while timidly asking you to dance. I found myself swooning with such standout lines as "I hear La Llorona with stars scraping over my head," and the more whimsical "His beard full of snarls and dead leaves, I wonder if birds nest there." Equipped with the descriptive powers of Allen Ginsberg, the rawness of Charles Bukowski, and the perspective of Dorothy Parker, Sarah Lilius is sure to enrapture and delight readers.

Georgia Park,
author of *Softly Glowing Exit Signs*

Sarah Lilius creates a world in DIRTY WORDS, born out of the tension between wanting to be saved from the grit and the necessity to peel oneself more profoundly into the fantasy ("to peel, a piece / of fruit, sweet girl"). This layering of tensions acts as a way for the speaker to become the monster so that we, the reader, can fight against it, feel liberation and freedom from it. It is in this freedom that the speaker becomes her own true hero. Emily Dickinson wrote that if she felt physically as if the top of her head were taken off, that's good poetry, and similarly, when that tension resolves between fleeing and digging deeper in this book's world, the top of the reader's head breaks into the sky. The speaker questions that "Maybe it's a game she needs / to play." And in a way, it feels as though this collection is "the movie / where the audience / looks away," but we aren't looking away. We take the hand of the girl who "use(s) (her) legs to break open the sky." We become the speaker's witness. It is a powerful rebirth story set in "a country / of pain" where "constellations draw / a map for her exit."

Shannon Elizabeth Hardwick,
author of *Before Isadore*

Dirty Words

Sarah Lilius

Havertown, Pennsylvania
United States of America

Copyright © 2021 Sarah Lilius

Cover design by Mitch Green
Editor: Kindra M. Austin

All rights reserved.
Printed in the United States of America.

"Dirty Words"

No part of this book may be used, stored in a system retrieval system, or transmitted, in any form or in any means by electronic, mechanical, photocopying, recording or reproduced in any manner whatsoever without written permission from the publisher, except in the case of brief quotations embodied in critical articles and reviews.

Published in the United States of America by Indie Blu(e) Publishing

For information, address
Indie Blu(e) Publishing
indieblucollective@gmail.com

ISBN: 978-1-951724-09-2

Library of Congress Control Number: 2021914610

For Matthew, Elliot, and Oliver,
who are always there with unconditional love.

Acknowledgements

Thank you to the journals where these poems first appeared:

Across the Margins: "The Weeping Woman Always Waits," "Hurry Sweet Violence," and "Ways I Drown"

Anti-Heroin Chic: "Frightened Girl in the Circus" and "A Young Girl Meets Her Older Self"

Arcturus: "The One Where Wifey Understands"

Bad Pony: "I Feel Stupid and Contagious"

Basil O'Flaherty: "A 25-Year-Old Girl Meets a Cat-Calling Man"

Biscuit Road Drive: "American Mother"

Blood Tree Literature: "Ode to Hole's *Live Through This*"

Boulevard: "Dirty Words"

Call Me [Brackets]: "West Point"

Coffin Bell Journal: "Departure"

Come as You Are 90s Anthology: "Thelma & Louise & Me"

Crab Fat Magazine: "Bear Violence"

Drunk Monkeys: "He Kills Butterflies"

Five 2 One Magazine: "An Ordinary Girl Meets a Man Living in a Tree"

Fourteen Hills: "Hotel Living"

Ghost Bible: "Haunting Me"

Gone Lawn: "Hearing Pearl Jam's *Ten* for the 115th Time" and "Becoming"

Hermeneutic Chaos: "Strange Domesticity"

Lumiere Review: "Weighing In"

The Massachusetts Review: "What the Masseuse Finds in the Backyard"

Melancholy Hyperbole: "Marriage on a Bad Day"

Menacing Hedge: "Milk Boy Carves a Glance from Glass" and "Mothers become mothers become mothers"

Moss Trill: "Holes," "womb walker" and "Women"

Pink Plastic House: "Plastic Soul Done Right"

Pithead Chapel: "Temporary in a dark purple Subaru"

Prong & Prosy: "Skin Tales"

Rabid Oak: "The Dissection"

Rag Queen Periodical: "The One Where I Change the End" and "Don't Let the Patriarchy Get You Down"

Red Paint Hill Poetry Journal: "Abortion Lament"

Red Savina Review: "No Oasis for Victims"

Sheila Na Gig: "We Were Birds"

Stirring: "The Stitching"

SLANT: "Finishing the Novel"

Thank You For Swallowing: "[ ] Culture"
Thirteen Myna Birds: "The Moment" and "XX"

Tinderbox Poetry Journal: "Better for Storms"

Window Cat Press: "A Girl Raids Her Wardrobe" and "A Lonely Wife Discovers A Trashy Girl"

Some of these poems appeared in the chapbooks, GIRL (*dancing girl press*, 2017), Thirsty Bones (*Blood Pudding Press*, 2017), and The Heart Factory (*Black Cat Moon Press*, 2016).

Contents

A Girl Raids Her Wardrobe 3
What the Masseuse Finds in the Backyard 5
The Weeping Woman Always Waits 6
A 25-Year-Old Girl Meets a Cat-Calling Man 8
Weighing In 10
The Dissection 11
An Ordinary Girl Meets a Man Living in a Tree 12
He Kills Butterflies 13
Finishing the Novel 15
Hotel Living 16
Hurry, Sweet Violence 17
The One Where I Change the End 18
The Moment 20
Ball and Chain 22
Bear Violence 23
No Oasis for Victims 25
Haunting Me 26
New Prostitution 28
Frightened Girl in the Circus 30
Koi Fish 32

Always	33
[ ] Culture	35
Skin Tales	36
Plastic Soul Done Right	38
Holes	40
XX	42
Abortion Lament	43
Dirty Words	45
womb walker	46
Strange Domesticity	47
The Stitching	49
The Medium Begins Her Night	50
Hearing Pearl Jam's *Ten* for the 115th Time	51
We Were Birds	52
I Feel Stupid and Contagious	53
Thelma & Louise & Me	55
what becomes when violent air lashes	56
Milk Boy Carves a Glance from Glass	57
West Point	58
Ode to Hole's *Live Through This*	60
Ways I Drown	61
Her Hair is Full of Crickets	62
Departure	63

Becoming 65
Mothers become mothers become mothers 66
Mother's Lament 68
American Mother 69
I'll Tell My Own Story 70
Better for Storms 71
Temporary in a dark purple Subaru 72
Marriage on a Bad Day 73
A Lonely Wife Discovers a Trashy Girl 74
Scene of a Woman Done 76
A Young Girl Meets Her Older Self 77
The One Where Wifey Understands 78
Don't Let the Patriarchy Get You Down 79
Women 80

Dirty Words

Sarah Lilius

A Girl Raids Her Wardrobe

A suit buttoned black, tight
as your mouth on Sunday,
store signs turn slow
on Saturday nights, walk home,
hand on mace, quick step matches
heartbeat on hell's banister.

A slinky red dress bunched up
and ready, who wears the garment
doesn't matter, young man/woman
with green eyes,
battered in luscious ways,
to sell, she or he, someone takes.

Comfortable concert T-shirts,
faded from constant wear
as a young girl, she wore
Nirvana's sloppy smile
for high school photos, black,
yellow, she could barely grin.

Clanking in big boots
trying to find answers,
she takes them off
only at night, the leather mimics
the sky, constellations draw
a map for her to exit.

Dirty Words

In skin, varied colors,
stretch in their sizes, monsters
hide in freckles, wrinkles, scars.
She's something to peel, a piece
of fruit, sweet girl, to eat and throw
away the seeds, the core.

Sarah Lilius

What the Masseuse Finds in the Backyard

I gave the devil a massage in broad daylight on hot summer grass. Skin on my palms began to burn and melt. Agony can feel good when it's wrong. His moaning lulled me, kept me in the dark place. We didn't dance but I assumed his pleasure formed inside me. Votive candles placed around the lawn sat effortless, immune to gusts of wind. We waited for the wax. He turned over to reveal a red, glistening chest, bare and toned. I poured and just for a second, I thought I saw something holy in his black and dilated pupils. What stared back at me was a country of pain, a place I related to. I packed up my supplies, we walked back to the house. I forgot to close my eyes.

Dirty Words

The Weeping Woman Always Waits

I listen to La Llorona
and think of you.

We kiss death until
I'm black in the eyes.

My feet, the bottom of my cotton
dress, are wet

but my hands are in the air,
dry as an accident.

There were two sons in my arms
now I'm left with a melody.

This song between my ears pulses
folk magic and dead, dead.

What concentrates on La Llorona,
different version like different loves,

catches the scent of a spice
I've smelled before.
I hear La Llorona with stars scraping
over my head,

pushing my hair gently away
from the madness that's become,

Sarah Lilius

that's residing in the bones of
beautiful women everywhere.

They skirt the dirty floor
with dreams of leaving.

Dirty Words

A 25-Year-Old Girl Meets a Cat-Calling Man

Smile, baby! (he whistles).
Look at those legs!
Hey, hottie, I'll buy you diamonds!

She looks down to the cracks
in the colorless sidewalk,
struts faster away.

Every day on her lunch break,
the man, the cigarette, crooked teeth,
dark jacket, acid washed jeans,
a nose too big for his face,

every day, he's there
calling her BABY, CHICK,
talking about her TITS,
her PUSSY. In this way,

he owns a piece of her,
her ether, her jumbled
non-reaction. He doesn't
speak of beauty,
he can't see her face.

Maybe it's a game she needs
to play, ask him about
his DICK, how it feels
in his pants when it rises

Sarah Lilius

to attention, about his MOUTH,
how his mother never taught him,
to keep it shut, odor and sound.

Weighing In

My body is a stifled boulder coated in olive oil then rolled around the dusty ground. I'm going to lose this fight with myself. Chemistry and biology and genetics. The fever of fatness covers the globe. I eat because I'm hungry. It's not good enough, there are not flowers on my table. The pounds take a moderately paced car to NYC and it's joyous for a time. I slip around like a snake after eating a rabbit. Digestion in a framework made for the metabolism of a lusty goat. I cover my face on the scale, naked, it's Saturday morning. Numbers are up. They are tattooed across my outer thigh. The black characters are ornately followed by shame. I tell myself that I don't care. My hands and feet are the smallest parts about me and that means happiness. A medium sized bone frame counts for something, right?

Sarah Lilius

The Dissection

I was cut into pieces
like cattle or a fat
pig that can't walk.

The men worked all night.
Blood everywhere.
The only noises came

from the saw and flesh
tearing. My head came off first
like a crown. Then limbs

before my meat with the special
names fell into their
red hands. Skin peeled back

like wet clothes.
I saw myself from above.
A moment they waited for, hungry.

Parts of my body roasted or thrown
to the other women, scraps to fight over,
I was never really over.
I lived on in the bellies of men,
the stomachs of ladies, who walked
around the dirt gathering instant gratification,
a fleshy fix, they pulled hairs
from slit mouths, still satisfied,
still unknowing.

Dirty Words

An Ordinary Girl Meets a Man Living in a Tree

His beard full of snarls and dead leaves,
I wonder if birds nest there.

He invites me up but the boards look
weather worn, surely uncomfortable
and I was never

good at climbing trees, my brother
had the tree house, stashed with porn
and special Kool-Aid.

My best friend, Mary, climbed there
once, only once.

The man picks his teeth with a small
bone, doesn't look me in the eye.

The frayed sign reads 294 days,
he speaks only to tell me,
he changes it every week.

I can see a scar across his bare chest,
just white enough to be called
yesterday.

Sarah Lilius

He Kills Butterflies

He kills butterflies
with bare hands.

Beauty snuffed out
by two swollen bowls

of skin, of callused
and red, always red.

The first time I saw
my eyes welled salty,

my ears imagined
a butterfly scream

delicate as wings
yet terrified.

He has no reason.
I turn to leave

with a flutter of legs
and a graceful show

of curls, of two eyes
tired of watching
the catch, the hard
squeeze and then

Dirty Words

the eager look on his face.
Nothing like those wings

midflight on a summer
day, nature's grandeur,

an insect revered.
I dream of beating wings

and the butterfly
is free.

Sarah Lilius

Finishing the Novel

When her eyes rest,
the letters of the words
pull apart like a lazy
couple caught in an affair
on a Tuesday afternoon.
His necktie is on the living room floor
spelled out like a message.
She drops her grocery bag of oranges
and Sprite Zero, heads to the bedroom
where outside the closed door
are magenta underwear looming
quietly on the carpet.
Her hand on the doorknob
is a change in tempo on the battlefield
of her marriage.
Everything ends and begins
as the door squeals open
slowly then crashes
against the dresser
where she keeps the things.
A handgun sleeps alongside
her tousled bras.
When her eyes fall down
to the floor,
the letters turn bright red.
A story worthy of dog-eared corners
and a toss of the book
against the closet
when the last sentence
is over.

Dirty Words

Hotel Living

At some point you're going to shower
in a hotel bathroom. You're going to turn
the water up, steam claiming the giant mirror
where you'll draw a crooked heart.

Clean won't matter to you. Stranger
pubic hairs, dark and wet, won't matter to you.
The dirty curtain touches your legs, it won't matter.

You'll probably order room service to see
the young man that brings it.
Maybe a Cobb salad with a Diet Coke.
Maybe not.

In the elevator afterwards, you will most likely flash
your breasts, two globes of sad light. The man will
look away. This isn't Mardi Gras.

Back at the hotel, you'll definitely find a human
tooth on the bathroom floor by the sink.
You'll place it in your mouth
and swallow.

Sarah Lilius

Hurry, Sweet Violence

This world looks like wedding cake, perfect little man/woman in their finest perched atop sweet icing. It was no accident when it fell to wood floorboards, bride and groom horrified, they place hands, faces against spongy goodness, purity in raspberry filling. There's nothing to find in layer after layer. Lurking music halts when the bride wails like a violin played by a child. We wait for the melody to settle into the air, a little lie. She walks fast against the dark sidewalk, her satin heels, white turns dirty. She waits for a catapult to throw rampage into her wavy hair, assault between her teeth, small bones, fast clenching pebbles in the darkness of her artful mouth.

Dirty Words

The One Where I Change the End

____ forces milk in my mouth, I purse and make a tight, pink O
    ____ manages, it opens and the white solid gags me, I'm no calf

(black out memory here)

____ takes me to his room, the basement air stiff, cold but unlike outside
    there's no open spaces to escape the closed door, the look of his face

(black   out   memory
    here)

then the bathroom floor in the dark, I turn the light off to hide
    I cry into the knees of my dark tights, my skirt crumbles around my weight

(here's where I change the end, no black out)

____ says he's sorry about the milk and that nothing happened to my body
    I remember the blankness and it's light, it's warmth against my face

Sarah Lilius

my best friend drives me home and we laugh
because boys, boys around
      our ankles, begging for another chance, silly
boys

The Moment

There is the moment,
cornered and heady.

I learn that a room can grow
small without magic.

A throb of walls,
windows push,
breath.

Amazing, the paint did not peel
from the heat
of my screams.

The mind tries to soften
the moment
with repression and vodka.

I doubt freedom
from the flashes
like lightning.

A terrible movie
where the audience
looks away.

His sour desire and awakened
strength—two pillars

Sarah Lilius

trying to separate.

He builds the moment
solid and silent,

this box of violence,
a rotting wood
I polish
like a lie.

Ball and Chain

I isolate myself in the living room, a female black bear without cubs to watch roll down hills of sharp summer grass. I let my mind dwindle into the past and I find him, passive boy I regret, I try to walk on the frozen lake, in the center, I fall in. He exists, an Illinois mystery I can't steal in my Subaru and question like a criminal, gun to temple, bat to knee. I paint his silhouette inside my body, the rare bird of violence and trouble, I want to hear his side desperately. The tattoos tell me nothing, just show colors that will fade, the lines form numbers and swell when he flexes and cries. How do I absolve what he did from my mind, no accountability on his boots, no grinding in his teeth.

Sarah Lilius

Bear Violence

Chews at my face, nose first, cheeks,
two red lips.

        Someone get me
handkerchief, tea towel, washcloth.

Blood won't scab, won't listen,
        to stop like a hardness eventually
becomes soft.

                I sit. I gather
evidence against you, and you, and him.

Dark open fields of lost replace
savage memories,

        the closed doors,
                the lights off, the way a
girl is gone,

hovers to don a grimace, bears loose
in the neighborhood, a body could
get mauled.
    So hide in the closet,
the bathroom, car trunk, until
you hear the shuffle, the slight
growl.

Dirty Words

        I don't want to ruffle
fur, let claws penetrate skin
and skin,   should I remember to heal?

Snippets let the pain
              in slow as a probe, looking

in my body for black nights,

                            no stars.

Sarah Lilius

No Oasis for Victims

Left naked in the desert
with a song in my head.
A cactus the only way to pierce my heart.
Repression is the sand around my feet,
after a while it stops burning.

Who knows where I'd be
if he hadn't dropped me here
like a parcel for someone else.
I never thought I'd be his problem,
a catalyst of violence and voodoo dolls.

He holds a pin for every day
and on Saturday there's extra.
Bits of hair, skin, drawn on eyes,
a serious doll, my mouth a straight line.
The stuffing comes out, he pushes it back.

On Sundays, when he goes to church
with his family in the air conditioning,
does he think of my naked body burning?
My dry mouth, the hurt between my legs
as he strokes his daughter's blonde hair?

Dirty Words

Haunting Me

He's dead as an answer.
The wood paneling of his basement
repeats without a sound.
Memory gaps like the space underneath
a short bridge.

I was once so young.
Now I can't remember how to do
up shoelaces.
My fingers break like a story
taking hold in the nighttime.

Everything has a face,
a thin body
that moves on the stairs
behind me effortlessly.
Shadows are structures
of ease and rainwater.

The delicate sound of red
and brown leaves, my scream
covered by a hand as the colors
hit cold pavement outside
the window.

I don't get away, but I try.
His pale skin testifies
and wins the prize.

Sarah Lilius

Later and always, a grand horse
trots from the barn.
That farm is where I live now.
The grass doesn't grow back
where it should.
A starving horse keeps my mind
On agony, on what's broken.

But the sturdy fence, a perfect rectangle, no gate,
splinters on my body, stays sturdy
like a man, in all kinds of weather
it's what never falls down.

New Prostitution

I sell myself
to a dead man.

Young man in a standard
coffin, brittle body

still contains the power
to cast me into his net of death.

He likes my blue veins.
My porcelain skin cells

are particle windows
ready to view.

Impossible whiteness
around my neck,

a place to whittle
desire.

One would think this
feels like elevator doors
opening to an empty car.
The satisfying ride
is the shape of your finger
pushing the six button.

Sarah Lilius

But slowness stabs
like a dump trunk full

on the interstate
moving towards

an exit it never finds.
Small pieces of someone's

day blow
across concrete.

In the satin-lined home
he insists on a closed lid.

Rain on earth
fools me

into finishing
the job.

Both hands tied
behind my middle,

I become the red lie
no one cares to hear.

Dirty Words

Frightened Girl in the Circus

Girl, use your legs to break open the sky

Whisper wind tells us not to fear what we can't understand

When the ice starts to fall, when the fire was lit

Girl, remember your heart isn't there for others to eat

Their gray fingers trace the size and place just right

Let them pick other organs first

And it's the bearded lady, the tattooed lady that get ahead

It's the clowns who win races that get applause

Girl, remember intuition will win you everything,

Tulips, two lips, lipstick red doesn't mean whore,

Raped anyway, fondled in the tent, stared at by a million eyes

Like all the pages in all the books, beauty is beauty, not for sale

Sarah Lilius

Girl, collect the bottles with all the pills, just in case

Keep the hard liquor in the old cabinet, just in case
Keep your elbows and knees sharpened, the ink,

The circus is in town and you can write on the tent,

Write your name, clear and black enough to

See from the sky.

Koi Fish

You might think I'm bait to my own sorrow. That I ask for your body to ravish my mind, to insert pain between my thighs, my source. You think I won't bounce into the pond and ride out what ails me like a small wave. There is sickness counting on me to thrive and feed it my eggs, the monster at midnight. And there are men, real, imaginary, shadow walkers, they harbor the spaces in my peripheral vision. My gills ache, my phantom legs are sore from pretending to run. Sometimes I dart, startle, but usually I turn the other way. I might leave the food pellet and swim to a new spot where the sun is a light on my parade of being brave, of answering your violence, like glass in my path, like nothing I can no longer see.

Sarah Lilius

Always

a man

          rushes
          towards me

to choke me,

     push,
         put his warm fingers

                       where it's
traumatized, hiding in slow
motion, a never dying plant.

It's breaking
          down anxiety in a forest

    of wrong.

    But I don't tell.

It circles me,   rewires me
                    like an
endangered thought

    crossing over the swaying bridge.

Dirty Words

Don't misstep,
      don't die
            all over again.

[ ] Culture

You're an animal
that feeds on media cookies.

You grow fat,
snarling from the cave

that's been created
for your violence to live.

Skin Tales

> *My body, that invisible body that girls keep.*
> ~Anne Sexton

Our skin cells, different
tiny animals than days
we were small girls, hairless
princesses with dirty skirt hems.

Barbie and Ken would do it,
plastic sex, a fast grind and drop
back to the tea party.

Barbie's blond hair
tragically knotted, unbrushable.
Mother would brush
my ratted hair, I would cry
as if this were the real violence.

Our skin cells, buffed
and soft in high school,
ready for touch,
in unknown basements,
we were teases,
keeping the prize hot.

All we found were hard-ons
on old couches, boys without condoms.
Boys found other girls,

Sarah Lilius

always willing to share
without smiles,
no real reflections
on their skin,
still tight, still smooth.

Dirty Words

Plastic Soul Done Right

Barbie always looks
      happy about it.

Barbie's lipstick
      never smudges.

She's a sentimental fool
      for a plastic man
           with no genitals.

She's not nostalgic
      about Ken's helmet hair
           molded in China.

Barbie's tight torso
      has no internal organs,
           no blood, no veins.

If your little brother
      cuts her hair, it doesn't
           grow back like a weed.

Barbie's rubber-feeling legs irritate
      those who try her pants
           on her pale scissors.

The threads can definitely wait
      for naked Barbie to get it together.

Sarah Lilius

We should question Barbie's
    vacant stare like the inside of a wall.
She's in her Barbie pink car driving nowhere,
    picking up no one.

Dirty Words

Holes

places
       I need to keep   in place, intact, no stretch, no bleed

my terms   I need to keep   my terms, my space, my body, all mine

the shaft   grows   thrives knives   tries

I see heart
      night stick
           what comes   what comes out

fresh fish   smell   like a secret
      coming down

find my clay   birds there find a nest
      warmth   to live

I leave within
      heat
          of myself   because   they take
      mine

Sarah Lilius

land of skin   honey   ocean
        dusty dusk

night of mine   let me lay   rest real   and
fire

                                                   the
clay

        necessary wetness

                                                   well
of my body, alive, mine

Dirty Words

XX

The girl as mini tragedy,
her smooth slit floats in the fluid,
ready for the cruel world,
ready to grow, bear her own children.

The girl is taken early from her mother—
two hearts beat through the procedure,
only one travels back home.
She will try again, he comes to her
                      every night.

The girl reappears like a trick.
Her hands are ready for work—
the cooking of rice and what meat
her family can afford.

The girl is taken again, no time
to be a spirit, no time to run the fields
in a thin dress, a hand me down
from another sister who never
                      existed.

Sarah Lilius

Abortion Lament

No woman wants an abortion as she wants an ice cream cone or a Porsche. She wants an abortion as an animal caught in a trap wants to gnaw off its own leg.

~Frederica Mathewes-Green

Tiny, they hang from the bare trees.
Silken cords around small necks,

no one wants to see a noose used for this.
Pink skin appears alive, smooth and vital.

I remember their lips, silent as fingernails,
and their hands brought to mouths as if to say *quiet, I just died*.

He wants to hide them like Easter eggs
but spring is late this year.

What a grim surprise for the children we let grow,
to let them find what's in the grass.
Blood and bone, nothing anyone wants on a resume.
It's a cracked highway we still have to travel.
Child—extension of my body, my body, my body.
My body's nobody's body but mine.
It's not a vessel to tie down,

Dirty Words

to get in and prod like a dead whale,

that beach, that sand.
I lay down and it's mine.

Sarah Lilius

Dirty Words

The words I find in the ground refuse to grow. Someone planted them here on purpose. They come out tangled like the barrel of monkeys game everyone hates when they're young. Letter by letter, noiseless, and shaped familiar against the light. I say out loud: *impossible, scarlet, scars, joint, ache,* and *burning violets*. Peculiar how they hang from my mouth, sounds become the air and then vanish. There's no one to hear my discovery. I brush the dirt off each letter with my hands. *Dirty words*. The rustling noise of my skin over the metal is inconsistent with the slight wind. When I hear the soft footsteps on the grass, I put my body over the letters. I cover them and they cut into abdomen through my shirt, ungrateful children fall back into the hole and they pull me away.

Dirty Words

womb walker

a bloody strut

      the double-sided uterus   a tool?   can't
win either way

      empty or full   bear the children
      no sweetness

               we will   LEGISLATE
     all of you   like

animals   like   space   we can rent

fallopian tubes   eggs   the nutrient rich
lining   the reason

we're   on fire   on trial   witches
    your wombs are walking

Sarah Lilius

Strange Domesticity

I've yet to see my mother slice
an onion, the white milky juice
seeps out like tears of a homemaker.

I can't recall my mother chopping
carrots for soup or stir-fry, long, orange,
hard enough to be a weapon.

When I was young, I remember
the laundry, the dishes, the cleaning
she kept up with so we wouldn't sneeze.

We were never dirty, *cleanliness is next
to Godliness*, she would joke
and laugh madly while wiping my face.

My room was kept neat as a folded
shirt, every fold sharp and proper,
every toy in place, rows of order.

My sister and I were her job,
the house, her job. My memories
are not vivid as she blended
into that house, the wallpaper she chose
for the hallway matched her new blouse
and there she lived, domestic chameleon,
someone I can't find
because she hides still—

Dirty Words

the floral pattern grazes her face.

The Stitching

We were taught to touch
patches of fabric with fondness
and reserve, to fear how soft
or how rough it could be.

When mother had her sewing needle
in hand, I thought she would sew up
my mouth, my skin,
make a place for me to survive.

When mother had her scissors
in hand, I thought she could cut
through glass so that we could
go outside, play in the street,
laugh at the other kids
in their faces.

Pins and needles grazed the carpet.
I never found them in my bare feet
but they would find a way
to my hands and prick me there.

The sewing machine was always
the loudest child in the house.
Grumbling to be fed the fabric
and thread, my mother's foot
pumping like it would save a life.

Dirty Words

The Medium Begins Her Night

This always starts out the same:
in the bedroom, dim air
penetrates my eyesight
and they come,
often shadows darker
than imagination
sometimes clearer
like a silent man
who stares at me,
I'm a piece of untouchable art
or an angry woman
who tries to take my child
right from the bed
where I smell nothing
like rotten fruit.
This is a parable
for everything
but I don't let religion
into my sleep space
for a little simple
story time.
I'm the editor
of my own heart.
It's terrifying to cusp
the spirits,
to understand
what isn't ever
to be understood.

Sarah Lilius

Hearing Pearl Jam's *Ten* for the 115th Time

We like the way this mixes us inside like germination, outside like spackling paste, messy perfect white. When curfew hits, an oak tree falls in our path. We didn't even notice the lightning until it was gone. The flash mistaken for a distant miracle. In the dark we fall, face to concrete, flesh to brick. Lilacs die from our stench.

I talk music with boys. The slightly cute ones with flannel or black everything, Chucks drawn on with Bic pens or Dr. Martens puddle muddied. Events shatter me like an abused cat, one eye torn out. I won't be the dirty girl again. I still fall on the ground weekly. Leaves convene in my hair like Bible verses in someone else's head. What victim has time for Jesus?

A strong melody like a bone I hold to crush the boys with dicks out. Their milky white songs are nothing I want to hear, radio never tuned to a sympathetic station. I can sulk or I can tighten my black boots, take to the burning sidewalk like it's yesterday, like it's nowhere I'll fall today.

Dirty Words

We Were Birds

For M

We were little girls, never seen
the ocean or a boy cry, never
seen the parts that would make us
mothers. Small secrets, we'd act
out scenes, we were birds, tiny chickadees
until unable to fly. Your cockatiel
landed on my scalp, now I always
duck when wings are present.
M, you were the sister I wanted,
even though I had an older.
You, an anchor to the village
we called home. Milan, Illinois,
nowhere near Italy,
nowhere diversity blossomed.
I kept secrets from you,
stones I held in my
extremities, cold as November.
Hands, feet cramped, months
of holding lead to pain.
Mornings, my disease grew
from what he did, we drove to
school, tired as buttons,
used over and over, a shirt
I threw out, long ago.

Sarah Lilius

I Feel Stupid and Contagious

My mind on a loop,
    stick my head in the leeching

past of the four-ring circus
    of Rock Island High School.

Distracted boys with knives,
    girls stroke boys' short black beards

with longing, hymens line up
    like nooses.

Cafeteria daze, I should have
    pills across my heart, rolling

in my blood like pigs, cut in half,
    there's never enough bacon for boys

with condoms in loose
    pockets. French fry pimples

keep boys from getting
    laid in father's minivans,
blue Hondas full of crumbs,
    fast food wrappers.

Musical trauma, we rock solid
    in the air, my gold Chevy,

Dirty Words

rolling tease wagon,
      I line up boys in flannel,

girl firing squad, self-control
      reeks of attitude and mint gum,

my Friday night fire
      kills when I drop

them off at spring curbs,
      grass newly green as us.

*Title taken from Nirvana's Smells Like Teen Spirit

Sarah Lilius

Thelma & Louise & Me

Thelma was a fast bird, the lucky one,
her character gets away,
gets revenge, gets farther
and farther away.

I can't tell you how I know
his hands would feel, hot steel
curved into bracelets, circles
misshapen like fried eggs.

I was a high school girl when
I saw that movie, still fresh, new.
A couple years later, my movie flashes,
scenes redone, dark camera low.

I can't say I'd shoot him,
there's a blankness there.
The cliff, that courage, an ashen
thing I'm still looking for.

Dirty Words

what becomes when violent air lashes

rape sits on the dresser
a dragon of full height
waits to release fire
watches with potent
and dilated eyes

rape lounges on the couch
cold ripped leather
scratches thighs on legs
of women who look
like me look like you

rape cooks on the stove
like a stew burning
carrot chunks too large
the rancid meat won't mull
in a pot falling fast urgent

rape rests in the bathroom
dirty thoughts excrete
into the filthy bowl
the cold water
with control and release

rape leaves in the car
only side streets for wheels
that roll like rough brambles
windows down ashes out
trunk full she's there

Sarah Lilius

Milk Boy Carves a Glance from Glass

Black cotton around knees, ankles, necks,
clothes he knows his mother will wash
after soiled with the names of the nameless.

Honey trapped in the container waits
for scalding tea that is just quiet water
searching for something to happen.

Hairs slight and blonde, tan freckles, counties
across the skin, he crosses the lines into new
territories, blood on the pavement.

The girl's barren memory, cross-stitched without
threads, the sayings of Jesus never reach
the pillow, the tacky wall hanging.

The girl's his white drink, fluid in darkness,
a noose swings, the oval, never quite finds a head
to place through, child skull and neck, never
tightens.

Dirty Words

West Point

Two words in my mouth,
                        hard ass   bad ass
     crazy ass,
     torn down the sides,
           reveals a real man.

I know you must have ruined
     your career when you left,   the person your father wanted you to be

     shattered into nights left closed.

Two words in his mouth
          yelled across a table   in a room
     your sister,   yourself,   your mother,
countless meals of no consequence.

Now your head is shaved.   Your boots.
    Your spine.
        Your hands hidden.   You're hidden.
Only new manhood   shows like a crease in camouflage.

I loved you.   I trusted you.   This ends badly.
    I write dumb poems about you.   Violent moments around my neck.

Sarah Lilius

    Push and silence as moving candles
    create mood,
               burn down houses.

I'm the mess you don't know
    you created.   One, two, three.
                        Turnstile
function,

    nothing left the field.
    Soldiers run home   daylight folds, moonlight
rips,   brides wait.
I'm in my mind   on a small bed
    waiting.

The way you ruined me
    like putting out a campfire, a firework gone
awry
               on your own personal holiday,
    now it looks patriotic,
        but it was always red, white, and blue.

Dirty Words

Ode to Hole's *Live Through This*

High school wooden gymnasium across
my filthy brain, I can't be sixteen again
but I can press play on the consistent current,
a jolt through the kitchen
as I slam dishes around in the dishwasher,
a machine I could call my bitch, washing the dirty
plates with the hottest water, it's a summer
heat wave in the box. I imagine bright pink
tongues finding delicious residue
and the skanky build-up on coffee cups.
I rebel and put the wooden handled chopping
knives in with the rest of the silverware.
Courtney rotates and curtsies around
the room I spend so much time in,
she growls, screams like a hearty act
of rebellion, a woman singing like that
and a last name like Love, is singular
yet plural, is a smudge, the whole canvas
with paint left over for your face.

Sarah Lilius

Ways I Drown

In the glass cube it seems irrational, speculative about why I'm in lukewarm water anyway. Liquid that's not warm enough when it enters my body through my mouth, personal cave. The bottom of two lungs is the end. Water that can't turn back. Stalled magic. I'm not mad. What I need to survive kills me every time. He can watch me through the clear walls. I'm a sour cocktail he sips then sets on a side table. I want to be an exception, to swallow the key this time, to just leave. This trick benefits the audience in their plush seats, popcorn on the floor. They never clap. They stare as the water drains onto the burgundy carpet. The solid glass box thumps to the stage and I'm dead another night.

Dirty Words

Her Hair is Full of Crickets

Her body, a flat stone,
she waits for other people
to rub the cool surface of her skin.

Her eyes are on video like a fluid lover,
she believes in social media, her best friend,
concrete, masked harpy keeps her up at night.

She can't wash her eyeballs, rolling up,
the rocks of overstimulation, grass over her skin
when she picnics with no one and everyone.

Insects, small mammals slay a nest
into her excessive hair, curls of forgotten
color, coarse tangent, unnecessary—

it grows not sturdy but like waves,
something others can't even hold
like dirt, like the answers of the earth.

She can't find the stream, to lie down,
drown the intruders, they make nothing
like noise, silence sews into her ears.

Sarah Lilius

Departure

Her heart passes through her
body like a stone.

The glistening muscle beats slightly
when she presses it to her chest,

the third newborn
she'll never meet.

Young and powerless, without a heart
she'll soon die over this hospital bed.

The white sheet already stained
with her effort.

Her blue patterned gown
torn at the hem.

Nurses step out to smoke
in the bathroom.

Labor was her own
pushing horse.

Through the snow lit box of a room,
mixed smell of bleach and people.

Alone, she waits to be greeted

Dirty Words

by the taker of the heart.

She imagines it will be a tall man
with crow dark hair but soft brown eyes.

The last man she will meet says nothing
but extends his gloved hands.

Sarah Lilius

Becoming

Biceps as wheels of the frame, strange and revolting, meat for cannibals or bears after the winter. They leave the cave one paw at a time; they find no sun against dingy fur. I cannot describe the fear mixed with calm about your biceps, about bears leaving caves. Moments of nature I could cut open with a spear if I was a hunter. I gather and it's absurd. Processed food and new sneakers. We often look for pools of chemical water but only in the summer. I want to see the forest again before I die. To look nothing in the gut, to find berries but not eat them because I've learned. Deep in the woods there's no gravel driveways, no lawns with plastic animals, or strange men rubbing themselves on sidewalks. I find grass to sleep on. Mother bear and her cubs sniff me, claw at my body, I am a body. Finally.

Dirty Words

Mothers become mothers become mothers

Infants fall like wet diamonds
from between my legs.

Built foot up, strong bones,
I'm made for this, I squat

over the linoleum, a world
of what specks have seen.

Blood tap taps then pours
as a pitcher of milk I will serve

them, content faces
watch me, I know

they are reflections
on the surface of time,

of the red on the slick
floor where they fell.

I scoop firmly, babies
who haven't cried yet

find blue in their passport
to this world, quiet entities.
Once they know to stay
is an option, naked wails

Sarah Lilius

rattle barriers, sort
puzzles back in place.

The sound of sometimes
and forever jolt a moment

into being, I'm part
mother, part monster.

Mother's Lament

I try to take care of them but it's like pulsing stars I'll never reach. The burning pinpoints of light are white, but I wonder, could they flash blue or yellow if they wanted to tell us messages of hope and grandeur. I try to keep them from the harm of our world but it's like the random icicle falling from the edge of our roof. That sharp point cuts into his body. Blood harbors inside his winter coat, sticky against the hot fabric. He still thinks icicles are interesting, beautiful weapons to hold in a mitten. Brothers in daylight around blinding snow. It's January. Just another day passes, and we call it a new year. New chances to swoop down and catch falling boys before they freeze in the newest snowfall, a microcosm of cold and boots sinking with a quiet crunch, a child noise they don't even hear.

Sarah Lilius

American Mother

Doesn't leave the house, the newest baby screams all night, all day. Colic thorns and her skin bleeds like a tattoo, the sound is a skull shape she slips into.

Loses it over dirty dishes, remnants of dinner float like greasy body parts, corn kernels are the yellowed teeth of her husband, a wet bread slice is his slippery tongue. His mouth overruns with unhappiness.

Quits her job to raise a boy, a girl, the accidental third. They crawl around her on the dirty carpet. The cheerful yellow vacuum is full. She cannot move to empty the canister. Bones, saliva, small heads keep her down.

Nested hair. Stretch marks. Slight body odor. Moldy shower. Toys imprint her skin. Spit up dries on her shirt in the shape of Texas. Nightly wine stains her teeth. Pounds heap on her ass. There's no sex.

Watches the laundry mountain sway, starts the machine with the teething baby on her hip, he bites her flesh like a diapered vampire.

Burns cartoons into her mind for a couple hours of sanity. They change over the years like her children, they lose interest, they speak, it's two blinks, a ride away from home, then over.

Dirty Words

I'll Tell My Own Story

A snippet here on Earth, I can barely
lift the pen to carve into the paper.
I think I'm more than speck or smudge.
I love the creature that holds up
the canvas with his muscular paws.
Opening doors over years
has me rife with slight wind
in my mouth, tussling my hair.
Departure is always complicated.
Once upon a time I was always
younger than the ocean.
My insignificant bones
keep me standing around
like I'm waiting for the next
child to choose me.
I hold up the furniture
with books I've read.
Knowledge is sturdy
with the sadness of the story.
My lines lithe,
they hold heaviness
like a house on the water.
The structure must sway
slightly, it constantly pauses,
waits for hurricanes
to show people
what endurance is,
what it can do
for them.

Sarah Lilius

Better for Storms

I let weather into me like a man.
I want thunderstorms to rattle my thighs.

The rain brings up the earth,
then the smell of childhood mud pies

and the way he looked at me
in the backyard, the bullets of a storm

changed to a drizzle where I could see
the water beading in his dark hair.

Newness changed into years,
we grow together, two saplings

that thrive resilient, hearty
roots long, deep, our clock circles

and now I've too much past
on my mind, in my dry hands

like a snake hissing
quietly as a threatened cat

in the dark hallway of the house I grew,
where I thrived into a woman and found

you could grow
your own ghosts.

Temporary in a dark purple Subaru

I am ready to catch car fire like a virus. I barrel around with nothing inside or everything inside. I resist becoming chores and runny noses. They say I must be a mama bear without the heavy fur. I carry around my empty honey pot in the trunk. I am words that rhyme with other words. What you can't scratch, a female dog sullen in heat. I'm in love with five different people. They have dark hair. They are collective. Some of them won't touch my skin. I'm coatless in the car seeping into the school parking lot. I wait for Monday to start the engine. I wait to see if reality steps in like a latte and I drink it down as if their names are on the side of the cup.

Sarah Lilius

Marriage on a Bad Day

My husband primes his straight razor.
I don't understand the strange paraphernalia
except for the silver blade
where our reflections frown.

Orchid roots stifle in a breakable pot.
Who shoots orchids like it's a gun range?
Can you even accurately kill the center?
The soft place every pollinator wants.

He won't kiss me on the mouth,
like he doesn't want what I have,
the intense way my brain captures
a moment like an execution.

Memories build themselves into
circles, like the rings we wear,
we resolve like a clean idea,
he shaves his face, his head.

Dirty Words

A Lonely Wife Discovers a Trashy Girl

She's the kind of girl
who snaps photos of her
naked body, fast, 100's
and then carefully chooses
the one where she looks ripest,

then sends pixels of her lust
to all the men she knows,
half the wives find the text,
hard nipples, soft hands across
an ocean of skin, it leads
to where half the men
want to go,

the stale smell of mall pretzels.
She lives alone, maybe
a cat she dresses
up for laughs, their fur
smells like cigarette smoke,
their fur mats and tangles.

She's caught in a snare
of non-existence, of the way
blood seems firm when
it arrives on her skin.
She cuts to forget
trailer park scenes, where
gravel imprints on her skin

Sarah Lilius

still surface, on bad days,
in the shower, her knees,
two false islands
that wait.

Scene of a Woman Done

I try not to let desire
hold me down.

My eyes, black
crow feathers

rest high
in neighborhood trees.

Every day, I'm the stance
of a woman who stares

into the sun constantly,
it's not even circular anymore.

My insides bitter
as unripe melons.

The violin background,
salt across my skin.

Turn down the symphony,
the instrument in my ear.

Regret is a sauce
spicy on my fingers.
I can't place liquid
down my body.
I leave the trail
for you.

Sarah Lilius

A Young Girl Meets Her Older Self

The first thing I notice are her smooth legs sticking out from her short dress like two long baseball bats. Her hair is like mine and she smiles too much, looks down at my dirty face, my wrinkled dress and suddenly frowns. I want to speak but can't form words from the mill of my mouth. I'm suddenly a wind stuck and I think she's going to smack me like our mother does, right across the cheek, it burns like I imagine acid would burn. My older self hunches like her shoulders are tired of being shoulders. Aren't bones supposed to be strong? I want to touch her high heel shoes, to see if I survive or if I turn into a puddle of future goo. Finally, she opens her red mouth to speak, *you smell like bubble gum and dirt*. I smirk and run off, ready to enjoy what time I have left.

Dirty Words

The One Where Wifey Understands

I am submission,
        a stone for you to rub and toss into the pond.
           I can't cut you out like a paper man,
stubble shouts with an eerie silence.

        Ghosts for hire in the backseat are those who listen
           so intently, they are catatonic air
from a window slightly open, mostly closed but always clear.

      I am the contents of your pockets,
         the jeans I wash because I have no job.
The clothes appear Copperfield style: I rarely see them
      removed.

        Our children, once the size of marbles:
I am done with smallness
    they continue outside my uterus to reach towards
        handsome manhood.

    I rub blood from my cut fingers across paper.
        The words find paths to each other,
white runways where letters trot with insecurity.
        I find a way alone: I am often myself.

Sarah Lilius

Don't Let the Patriarchy Get You Down

My body changes,
    I lather up my own history
        over and across,
            a waning river pulls down.

        The rocks are silent as guns,
    never shoot. I'm unzipped.
I'm tethered, I'm the bride in black.
My wet boots keep

my feet stomping around
    an earth we can't give them
        anymore, where are you
            Goddesses? No lace, no sequins,

        really, no desire to mate.
    We're the tree and the roots,
take it down, fashion a table,
lay him down. Payback

    with tiny needles, keep it legal, legislate his body.
But let it bleed.

Dirty Words

Women

We roll our eggs gently across dirty floors
      We throw the eggs on dirty floors,
      watch them crack like a life

We use our bones to gather children
      We mend our bones broken with time and balm, the open air

We use our muscles to clean the messes
      We rub our muscles against the machine, it grinds like love

We are painted like whores
      We are painted with warrior blood because we   choose to fight

We asked for it
      We never asked for it, the violence between our   legs

We, underpaid, over stressed,
      We cannot walk in the dark

We ask for compensation and lakes with boats, herons
      We clutch, we watch, we are bodies of crescent   shaped reality

Sarah Lilius

We walk at midnight under a moon
      strapped to the sky's darkness

We keep taking back the night, but they still take us
      under water
      We take back the night, it's ours to tuck under
our   skirts

We are dressed inappropriately
      We killed the rooster because we didn't like
his   strut

We drink the drink, we watch hands come for our
faces
      We are thirsty, we make mistakes

We are silenced, when you're drowning—is there
any   other way to be?
      As the gavel drops—
      we open our mouths

Sarah Lilius is the author of five chapbooks including GIRL (dancing girl press, 2017) and Traffic Girl (Ghost City Press, 2020). Her sixth chapbook, Song for PTSD, is forthcoming from Blanket Sea Press. Dirty Words is her first full-length poetry collection. Some of her past publication credits include the Denver Quarterly, Court Green, Fourteen Hills, Boulevard, and The Massachusetts Review. She has been nominated for a Pushcart Prize and a Best of the Net Prize. She grew up in the Midwest but now lives in Virginia with her husband, two sons, and their cat, Ophelia. Her website: sarahlilius.com

Another Indie Blu(e) Title You May Be Interested In:

Crimson Skins
Devika Mathur

Devika Mathur's haunting, visual work speaks of imagined journeys and freedoms, through imagistic and richly textured poetry. Her work challenges the accepted notions of the female, and illustrates the intensity and eloquence of her life.

https://www.amazon.com/Crimson-Skins-Devika-Mathur-ebook/dp/B08GCWK4D5

Another Indie Blu(e) Title You May Be Interested In:

SOFTLY GLOWING EXIT SIGNS

Georgia Park

Softly Glowing Exit Signs is a photo album of a life lived intensely and painfully, but really lived, and survived. Georgia Park is a woman growing up through these pages, into a survivor, someone you want to know because she's damn clever, fiendishly smart, and desperately real.

https://www.amazon.com/Softly-Glowing-Exit-Signs-Georgia-ebook/dp/B085N19ZFX

Another Indie Blu(e) Title You May Be Interested In:

THE LITHIUM CHRONICLES
Nicole Lyons

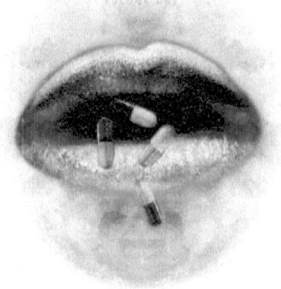

Nicole Lyons' poetry and prose are wholly relatable, taking us deep inside the heart, and the human condition. Unafraid to bare her soul, she shares her struggles skillfully crafted with every line, giving the reader permission to take a glimpse into their own.

Volume I
https://www.amazon.com/Lithium-Chronicles-One-Nicole-Lyons/dp/1732800049

Volume II
https://www.amazon.com/Lithium-Chronicles-2-Nicole-Lyons/dp/1951724011

Indie Blu(e) Publishing is a progressive, feminist micro-press, committed to producing honest and thought-provoking works. Our anthologies are meant to celebrate diversity and raise awareness. The editors all passionately advocate for human rights; mental health awareness; chronic illness awareness; sexual abuse survivors; and LGBTQ+ equality. It is our mission, and a great honor, to provide platforms for those voices that are stifled and stigmatized.

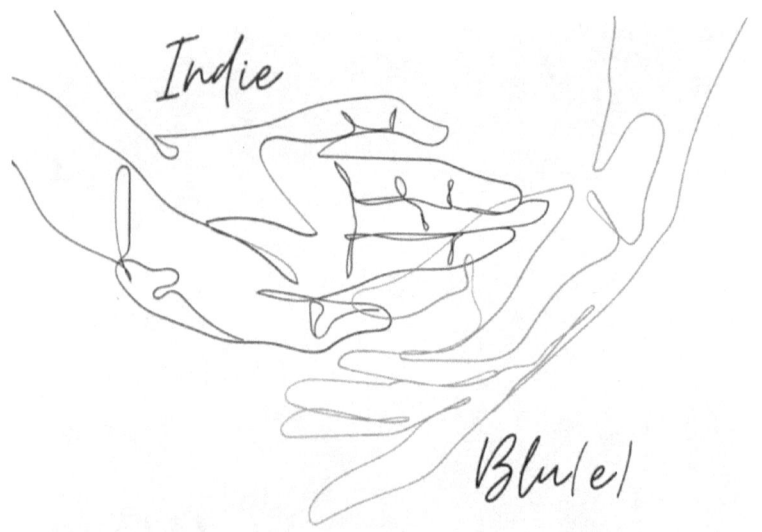

Indie Blu(e) Publishing wants your best and most incisive work. We are welcoming to all artists/writers regardless of race, orientation, gender, gender expression/identity, body type, ability, religious beliefs, income, or immigration status. We are actively seeking submissions from under-represented voices, including artists/authors who are Black, Brown, women, indigenous, gender-nonconforming, people with disabilities, lgbtqia+, and neurodivergent.

We will not accept/publish pieces that depict gratuitous violence, racism, sexism, homophobia, transphobia, xenophobia, and/or hate speech.

www.ingramcontent.com/pod-product-compliance
Lightning Source LLC
Chambersburg PA
CBHW022010120526
44592CB00034B/772